IMAGES
of Wales

CENTRAL
BRIDGEND
AROUND ELDER STREET

Bridgend Civic Trust

In early 1993 Bridgend Town Council decided that something must be done to improve the Town and its environs. They decided that a pressure group was what was needed and they enlisted the help of the Civic Trust for Wales. At a public meeting in March a small steering group was formed to start the ball rolling. After several months of deliberation and planning the steering group decided the following:

To form a branch of the Civic Trust in Bridgend

Design a logo for the group

Compose a mission statement

Decide on an issue to set the ball rolling (traffic management in Bridgend).

At a well attended public meeting in November 1993, the branch was formally launched to general acclaim. Since that time it has been active in publishing a twice annual newsletter, holding public meetings, pressurising the councils and bringing issues to the notice of the public. (Charles Thorp)

'The Bridgend Civic Trust will promote a higher quality of life for the people of Bridgend. The Trust will encourage high standards in planning and urban design and facilitate the involvement of the community in the planning process. It will take practical steps to promote environmental understanding and civic pride in the town and will seek to work in partnership with the local authorities and other relevant agencies to achieve its goals.' (Mission statement)

IMAGES
of Wales

CENTRAL
BRIDGEND
AROUND ELDER STREET

Natalie Murphy

in association with

TEMPUS

Ethel 'Polly' Jenkins (*née* Tee), the grandmother of the author, (1875-1962). She lived at No. 3 Elder Street for nearly sixty years.

First published 1996, reprinted 2005

Tempus Publishing Limited
The Mill, Brimscombe Port,
Stroud, Gloucestershire, GL5 2QG
www.tempus-publishing.com

British Library Cataloguing in Publication Data.
A catalogue record for this book is available from the British Library.

ISBN 0 7524 0690 6

Typesetting and origination by Tempus Publishing Limited.
Printed in Great Britain.

Contents

One of a collection of pen and ink drawings showing Elder Street as it would have looked in the late nineteenth century. It was drawn by local artist Alan Saunders.

Caroline, Dowager Countess of Dunraven, a lady who was very generous to Bridgend.

Introduction

By Hilary M. Rowley

Over the years several books have been written about Bridgend, but this is the first to concentrate on the heart of the town which links the hamlets of Newcastle and Oldcastle.

The development of the centre revolves around Elder Street – originally the main coaching route to the Ship Inn and Wyndham Hotel – and Dunraven Place (High Street), spreading up Market Street (Union Street), Adare Street, Wyndham Street and Caroline Street. Paradise Street, along with others, has been lost without trace.

It is believed that the first street took its name from Elder House, which stook on the site now occupied by Family Value. Union Street was renamed when the cattle market moved from the area of Adare Street to the site of the present bus station, and Lady Caroline renamed the other four streets after members of her family and her estate in Ireland.

Through the ages Bridgend has undergone many changes, but none as dramatic as those that took place between 1960 and 1980. During this period of purging, many valuable amenities and historical sites were demolished in the name of progress. The most important ones were:

The Town Hall – an imposing landmark and a place that holds many happy memories for me. It provided a venue for dances, exhibitions, and theatre companies. Paintings that had been donated to the town by well known dignitaries and artists were on permanent view. The lesser hall provided facilities for meetings and jumble sales.

The Market Hall, in Caroline Street. Built on the site of the older open air market, it combined character with usefulness. Annual eisteddfodau were held in this building from 1906 to 1939, as well as other musical events.

In 1987 the last of Bridgend's four cinemas was converted into the Ritz Bingo Hall. The loss of the 800-seater County Cinema, in Cross Street/Elder Street, in 1980, will also be regretted for many years to come. This cinema, built with full theatre amenities, could have provided a 'culturally deprived' town with a centre for live entertainment as well as a cinema. Our long established Bridgend Castle Players, who now have to rehearse and perform at Nantymoel, would have had a home base.

It was seeing the wanton demolition of buildings, which provided important facilities for the town, and their replacement with inferior substitutes, or empty spaces, that prompted Natalie Murphy to collect and record Bridgend's disappearing history. This book is a testimony to her hard work. The story of the town and its personalities is told through photographs dating from the turn of the century to the present day.

I first met Natalie when she was researching Elder Street and discovered that not only did we share a connection with this area but also the same ancestors.

Bridgend is once again undergoing considerable 'development', for example with major road works in process and Bridgend Civic Trust are pleased to see a record being made of what the town once looked like. We also look forward to the renovation of the much neglected Elder Street which will link the past with the present. Unfortunately, No 1 – last used as a Chinese Laundry and previously as the Red Lion public house burned down in 1994. Next door the former Court Bakehouse still stands but in a sad state of repair.

The successful Saturday pedestrianisation of Adare Street, which commenced in 1973, has failed to mature into the long awaited full-time closure, as was promised. The Bridgend Civic Trust has fought hard for this street to be pedestrianised throughout the week, but so far to no avail. Maybe new strategies for the development of the town centre will redress this problem.

I hope that this book will stir interest in both the past and the future of Bridgend. In the past it was the need of the people that shaped the town. Today we have another opportunity to help reform the heart of Bridgend to suit our present day and future needs. We must not let this opportunity pass us by.

Elder Street looking west, 1980. The telegraph pole in the distance was at one time the tallest in the town. In the 1950s twenty feet was taken off the top for safety. The white building on the right has in its time been a department store, tax office and job centre. On 23 August 1929 it was reported that 'an 'expert' had declared that 'it was about time that Bridgend Council set about repairing Elder Street because the volume of 'Presbyterian' traffic in that thoroughfare was constantly on the increase'! (*Glamorgan Gazette*).

One
Families of Elder Street

Maria Griffiths, outside the Red Lion public house in Elder Street, c. 1920. Robert Griffiths, his wife Maria and daughter Natalie, moved from the Five Bells public house in 1916. Robert was paid 25 shillings a week and a further 8 shillings for one servant. The pub was owned by the local brewery, R.H. Stiles on Tondu Road.

William Sutton (standing), his wife, Mary, his two younger sons, Clarence and William, and daughter, Maude (the seated man is unidentified). After some years running the Red Lion, the family moved back to Australia leaving behind the eldest son, Percy, who was by now was an apprentice saddler (see p. 119). The Red Lion was erected in the 1850s by George and Joseph Lill; their widowed sister, Mary Singer, ran the pub for many years, together with her second husband, Walter Brewer, whom she married in the late 1860s.

Ted and Mary Mayo, the last landlord and landlady to keep the Red Lion. They arrived in 1929 and kept the licence there until the brewery sold the pub in 1936. The R.H. Stiles brewery on Tondu Road was itself sold to H. & G. Simonds in 1938. Polly Jenkins is seated (right) and Winnie Jenkins (front), c. 1920.

The Jenkins family, No 3 Elder Street, 'The Bake House', 1915. From left to right, Sybil, Bert, Winnie, Jack, and baby Mollie.

Mollie (centre), Charles (right) and the youngest of the seven Jenkins children – one-year-old Nancy, 1919. At the age of twelve, Nancy took over a paper round from her brother Charles and for two years was the first and only girl in the town to deliver the *South Wales Echo*. On Saturday evenings she also sold the *Football Echo* in the vestibule of the Cinema.

This photograph, taken in the middle of the 1930s, shows a now grown-up Jenkins family. From left to right: Charles, who joined the RAF and became a rear gunner in the Second World War, Mollie, Gran (Polly), Nancy and Grandpa (Harry). The child in the front is Cynthia, the eldest of Polly and Harry's seventeen grandchildren. Standing at the back of the photograph is Jack, who joined the Welsh Regiment and became a 2nd Lieutenant. Sadly, he was killed in October 1944 while on active service in Holland.

Joe Lodwick in his uniform during the First World War. Joe, his wife Annie, and two sons, Bertie and Leslie, lived at No 5 Elder Street. Joe was one of the first men to work for the AA (Automobile Association).

Esther ('Etty') Bowen (*née* Evans) in her garden at No 7 Elder Street, 1930s. She married William Bowen in 1919 and they had four children: Billy, Marion, Gwyn and Dillwyn. William together with two of his sons, Billy and Gwyn, worked at the Gas Works on Quarella Road.

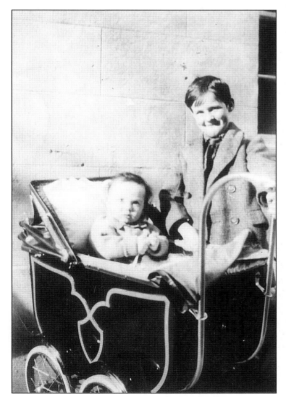

Dillwyn (in pram) and Gwyn Bowen, outside No 7 Elder Street, mid-1930s. Together with Billy, the brothers were affectionately known as the 'Bowen Boys'.

Bert Jenkins, aged about twenty, with Gordon Hopkin who lived at No 6, c. 1929.

Although there are no photographs available, mention should be made of Margaret Price and her daughter, Maggie Anne Price, of 10 Elder Street. On market days mother and daughter opened their tiny front room as a tea-room offering hospitality to farmers' wives and their friends for afternoon teas. During the school term, lunch hours were also spent there by the young ladies from the Bridgend Preparatory School.

Gladys and William ('Johnnie') Griffiths of No 9 Elder Street. c. 1915.

14

The Hopkin family of No 6 Elder Street. Tom and Mary Hopkin are pictured in this studio portrait from the 1920s with their six children, Gordon, Dilys, Gwyneth, Dick, Clifford and Violet. Tom was an accomplished musician, playing the piano and singing on special occasions at the Cinema.

Joe Redman, in the 'Wyndham Yard', *c.* 1920.

Brothers Frank and Billy Redman, *c.* 1920.
The boys belonged to the Hope Church Scout
Troop.

Joe and Emily Redman with four of
their children, Nesta, May, Violet
and Jack, at the rear of their home
at No 11 Elder Street, *c.* 1925. The
Redman family moved to Elder
Street from Coity around 1916.

Left: Charlie Pennell in the back garden of No 12 Elder Street, 1920s. Charlie and Mabel Pennell moved to Elder Street about 1912 and their two daughters, Mary and Olive were born at No 12. Charlie did not like the changing times, so when electricity was installed in the street *c.* 1920, he refused the offer of this new power for his house. Mabel remained living at No 12 until her death in 1983, aged 90 years, with no electricity, no gas, no inside toilet and no bath room. Right: Mary and Olive in the mid-1930s.

Jenny David and, to her right, her husband Bill. Jenny and Bill David arrived to live in Elder Street in the early 1940s, They lived firstly at No 8 and then, because of the redevelopment of Elder Street/Cross Street, they moved into No 14. Mrs David died in 1993. She was the last person to live in Elder Street.

This photograph shows one of the many family outings to the sea-side with the Mayo family from the Red Lion, the Jenkins family, Bob Morris from the Ship Hotel, and Betty and David Jones from the White Lion public house in Adare Street, *c.* 1930.

'The Local Boys' photographed in Elder Street with the Wyndham Yard in the background, early 1930s. From left to right, standing: Jack Jenkins, Griff Loveluck, Bert Jenkins, Ches Parkin (he became a local councillor). Middle: Spencer Mayo. Bottom: Bobby Mayo and Bob Morris from the 'Ship'.

Coronation day, June 1953. The Elder Street 'Queen', Anne Hopkin, was crowned by my grandmother, 'Polly' Jenkins. The two attendants were myself Natalie Gibbs (left), and Jennifer Rees from Adare Street. The celebration tea was then held in the loft of the chapel of rest.

Coronation of King George VI in May 1937. The celebrations were held in the 'Wyndham Yard'. Amongst the children are the Bowen family, Roy and Joan Dunlop and the Gray brothers. The ladies standing at the back are Mrs Dunlop, Mrs Greg and Mrs Beattie Hopkin.

Two
Elder House
and the Lloyd family

This eighteenth century house was completely hidden in the town centre and was quite possibly a coaching inn in the main thoroughfare through the town. The house was accessible through a large arched wooden door in a high stone wall, built of local limestone. The thick sash windows had indoor shutters that were closed with iron bars while the front door was graced by a knocker in the shape of a Napoleonic eagle. The door opened onto a large stone-flagged hall and there was a dining room on one side and a drawing room on the other. To the rear of the house was a large kitchen/breakfast room with adjoining pantry. A cast-iron stock pot was always kept on the coal range. Electricity was installed in about 1912. Mrs Lloyd did not mind having candles in the drawing room but electric light was needed in the kitchen and down in the cellar. The first floor had five bedrooms (four large ones with grates and one small room). There was also a bathroom converted from a bedroom. This room also had a grate. Above, on the third floor, were two attics and a large box room running the length of the house. Here the girls slept. Down below was the cellar with limestone block floors. Heavy Welsh slate slabs ran at waist level on two sides. There was also a stone cheese press, hooks for hanging up hams in the ceiling and two meat safes made of wood. The ceiling of the cellar was always cool even in the hottest weather because it was below ground level. A shaft with a window that could be closed in cold weather emerged into one of the garden flower beds. Outside were various buildings: a pigsty, stables and a building with a loft above. In the latter there was a water tap and a constant supply of spring water, which was always cold and never ran dry. This was a godsend when the mains water was cut off for any reason. A narrow passage, unsuspected by most people, ran from the rear door of the house between the buildings and out into Derwen Road. To the right of the house was a factory-like building, badly damaged by fire in 1914. This housed the wholesale side of the 'Bevan & Lloyd' business. The Lloyd children were evacuated from the house for the night for fear of flames spreading to the house. However, the house escaped the fire. (Reminiscences of the Lloyd family)

The Lloyd family in the front garden of the 'Elder House', summer 1923. From left to right: Anne, (Nancy) Kitty, Marjorie, Mrs Annie Lloyd (*née* Tanner, formerly matron of the old Cottage Hospital), Mr Leoline Lloyd, Bertie and Phyllis. Sadly, in 1960, the once beautiful 'Elder House' was demolished to make way for the very modern Co-operative store.

Leoline and Anne Lloyd with their five children, summer 1923. This portrait was made by local photographer and artist, Edwin Lott.

Kitty, the tomboy of the Lloyd family and a keen gardener. Kitty would don a pair on man's dungarees which was a very daring thing to do in those days when women never wore trousers and jeans were not invented. Kitty learnt to drive a car at the age of 16 and remembers, just before going to London in 1926 to train as a nurse, driving a 'Bevan & Lloyd' lorry, with a man as a bodyguard, to transport goods to the coal-mining valleys during the General Strike.

From top: Marjorie, 'Kitty' (Kathleen), Phyllis, 'Nancy' (Anne), and Bertie, c. 1926. The family had moved to 'Elder House' in 1912, when the youngest child (Bertie) was expected. After a very happy childhood at the house, the children left in turn to pursue their careers – the girls to train as nurses and Bertie to study law.

From the left: Bertie Lloyd, Cecil Jones (who later became the Revd Cecil Markham-Jones) and Fred Fear. This photograph was taken at the rear of Elder House. All three boys were very much involved with the Hope Church Scout Troop.

L.O. Lloyd and staff outside Bevan & Lloyd, Caroline Street. c. 1902. At the end of the nineteenth century, Daniel Herbert Lloyd arrived in Bridgend and was befriended by Mr Hugh Bevan who owned the grocery shop (above). Mr Bevan took the young Daniel into his business and in due course made him a partner. The business expanded considerably and when Mr Bevan died he left the business to D.H. as he was called. Leoline Oscar ('L.O.') Lloyd, being Daniel's eldest son, was encouraged to enter the family business.

The upper floors remain as they were when they housed apprentices to the grocery trade on the ground floor. They were looked after by a housekeeper. Much of the apprentices' work was to measure out and pack quarter-pounds, half-pounds and pounds of tea into special bags. The tea arrived in chests from India, Ceylon and China. To the right of the picture is the Castle Hotel/Inn. This had incorporated a corner toll house. The toll gates, however, which had been positioned on the right and left of the toll house, had long since disappeared by the time this photo was taken.

Bevan & Lloyd, Derwen Road, winner of the best-dressed window in 1937. The children, from left to right: Mervyn Davies, Pat Davies (a cousin) and Brinley Davies. The boys' father, Cliff Davies, was manager of the shop at the time.

Remains of a scout hall in the grounds of Elder House, probably part of the Bevan & Lloyd warehouse, early 1960s.

Three

Wyndham Yard
– the way it was

Prominently placed in Wyndham Yard were the chapel of rest and the garages. Both formerly stables, these structures were all built between 1865 and 1870 with limestone and sandstone although unlike the cottages, the stable walls were left unrendered. Steps were laid to the first floor loft cum workshop where coffins were hand-made at the time. One access only existed to the chapel of rest via a secluded doorway situated to the rear of the undertaker's office. The outside door belonged to the first Hope Church in Queen Street. In those halcyon times, on the day of the Bridgend cattle market, farmers would leave their horses and carts in the cobbled yard, while they went off to the mart. What a wonderful echo resounded across the yard as magnificent animals were freed from the cart shaft to amble over the cobbles to the stables. Quite often these horses would be accompanied by beef cattle and milking cows, the latter, of course, much to the delight of the local families living in Elder Street, who would greatly relish the opportunity of receiving fresh, creamy milk for their home larder.

That a travelling circus regularly visited Bridgend (the big top being sited at either Brewery or Stiles fields) would also certainly generate much interest and excitement with the Elder Street people (particularly the younger 'Elders') since the troupe's elephants would be well catered for at the Yard stables.

A menagerie of livestock indeed! However, such fascinating visits were not made just by animals, for during the summer months, the 'onion men' from Brittany in France would be made just as welcome at the Yard. Two regulars, bedded in the loft, were the warmly remembered 'Francis' and 'Allan', both of whom were well received despite speaking very little English.

Sadly, the 'garage' section of the old stable, which was 'L' shaped and once housed a saddle room and blacksmith's shop, was demolished about 1982, while the chapel of rest survived a little longer until 1990.

The yard and garages of Messrs. E. Morgan and Sons, Funeral Directors, January 1977. The garages were once the stables of the Wyndham Arms Hotel.

Edward Morgan, founder of E. Morgan, Funeral Directors, mid-1920s. He had begun at Hermon Road, Caerau, Maesteg in 1899, with his horse-drawn carriages serving local funeral directors and carrying out contracts for the GPO delivering mail to the valleys of South Wales. In 1912, he moved with his sons to Wyndham Yard and started in the undertaking trade. After seeing active service in the 1914-18 war, the sons Arthur, Trevor and Emlyn rejoined their father in the business. 1922 saw the introduction of the motor car into the firm, which continued to flourish under the direction of Edward Morgan. Following his death in 1952, his sons continued to expand the business in the Bridgend and Mid-Glamorgan area. Trevor, Emlyn and Arthur died in 1961, 1962 and 1963 respectively and the firm was then joined by Mr Cliff Jones and Mr John Greenslade of Griffiths & Jones. E. Morgan and Sons finally closed its doors in Elder Street on 5 November 1990.

Trevor Morgan in the yard, *c.* 1940.

Wyndham Yard, late 1950s.

Emlyn Morgan and an unknown gentleman, photographed in the yard around the early 1920s.

Arthur Morgan, Nellie Griffiths (in Welsh costume) and Nellie's sister Hetty from Hamilton, Ontario, Canada, 1920s.

Owen Griffiths at the wheel of the car with Alec Holloway, *c.* 1918. Owen's two children, Gladys and Johnnie are in the back.

Owen Griffiths and 'Chippy' Holmes are seated in the front with brothers Trevor and Emlyn Morgan behind, mid-1920s. Owen Griffiths worked for the Morgans at this time, living next door at No 9 Elder Street. He later moved to Green Street to run his own funeral business.

'The Brittany Onion Men', 1920. Standing, on the left, is Trevor Morgan and kneeling in front of him is Joe Redman. Standing extreme right is Arthur Morgan and just below him is Billy Redman.

Four

The Cinema and Cross Street

Description of the building as reported in the *Glamorgan Gazette* of 3 May 1912:

'The new electric theatre being erected by Mr Jacob Jenkins is eagerly looked forward to by the people of Bridgend and neighbourhood. We are informed that the proceeds of the first performance will be given to the Cottage Hospital and other local objects deserving of charitable support, and this alone should be the means of filling the spacious theatre to overflowing. The work is sufficiently advanced to enable one to see what a fine hall the town will possess and to realise it will fill a long felt want for the district. The site is a central one, the front of the building facing Cross Street, and the whole scheme has been so planned as to give the greatest comfort and convenience to patrons. Access is gained through a central archway, the leading feature in the front elevation to a semi-circular vestibule, and thence through the doorways to the body of the hall and by means of a wide and easy stairway to the dress circle and upper gallery and cloak-rooms. Attention is immediately drawn upon entering to the fine proportions of the hall, and to the pleasing effect of the internal decorative scheme. The main hall from vestibule wall to the proscenium front has a length of 73 ft and a width of 40 ft, and the height from the floor near the stage to the centre of the curved ceiling is 33 ft. Careful provision has been made to ensure an uninterrupted view of the stage from all parts of the house, the floor of the auditorium being constructed with an ample slope and the dress circle arranged in tiers. Accommodation is provided for about nine hundred people. The body of the hall and the dress circle is sumptuously fitted with velvet covered tip-up chairs. One of the features of the theatre is the fine stage, 40 ft by 20 ft, arranged on modern lines and having all requisite fittings for the production of plays. Ample dressing room accommodation is also provided for both artistes and members of the orchestra. The entertainment to be provided will be on high class lines and the pictures the best thrown from projectors of the latest type. The safety of patrons has been very carefully considered, the projector room being isolated and fire-proof, [although in the middle of the 1920s, a small fire broke out in the projector room, causing minor burns to Frank Redman, the projectionist] and ample exits provided from ground floor and galleries. The general idea of internal decorations is based on recessed arcading and niches for the side walls, and bold ribs and decorated panels in the ceiling. The whole scheme has been admirably executed to the architect's designs and the finished decorated plaster work is without doubt some of the finest in this style of building…
'…The proscenium opening is 23 ft wide and 18 ft high and has an elliptical arch moulded and enriched with a bold treatment of laurel leaf decoration and the whole being surmounted by a cornice with medallions and chrichments and pediment curved to sweep of ceiling. The large centre ornament over the proscenium is a handsome cartouche, with festoons of flowers and fruit and having a plume of feathers as crest. The recessed arcading of the side walls is formed with panelled pilasters leading up to ceiling ribs, and having moulded enriched capitals and cartouches with flowers and fruit decorations continued in trails down the face of the pilasters. The arched recesses between these pilasters have richly modelled capitals and key blocks, and the spandrels above the arches are filled with wreaths of flowers and sprays. The niches in the lower part of the panels formed by the arcading are intended for statuary, and have beautiful modelled semi-circular shell ornamented coved heads, the side panelling being

'The Cinema', August 1912. The ornate plaster work was hand-moulded by master plasterer Alfred Adsley.

(from previous page) decorated with sways of flowers and fruit. The front of the circle is treated with festoons of laurel. The ceiling panels formed by the main curved and moulded ribs are decorated with curiched and moulded plaster work and patarae and have large circular pierced ornaments as central features in each panel. These central ornaments serve as ventilating outlets and are connected with powerful electrically driven fans by means of tubing. The colour scheme of decoration has been beautifully carried in soft shades and shows great skill and refinement in its treatment. Ivory white and pale reds and gold being the leading tones throughout. Heating will be by means of gas-generated steam radiators and ventilation by fresh air inlets in recesses behind the radiators and exhaust extractors in roof as previously noted. The whole of the general construction has been carried out by Messrs. Charles Jenkins and Sons, Bridgend under the personal supervision of Mr Jacob Jenkins, and they have been well served throughout by the foreman in charge, Messrs Jones and Norman. The heating scheme has been carried out by the Bridgend Gas and Water Co., The Electrical Wiring and Accessories Co., Aberdare. The Tibraus plaster work and colour decoration by Messrs. D. Jones and Co. Ltd of London. Mosaic floors and steps by the Marble Mosaic Co. of Bristol; Collapsible gates by the Bostwick Gate Co.; Stage fittings and tip-up seating by Messrs F. Wilkins and Bros. of Liverpool; Carpets and other furnishings by Mr T. Edwards of Bridgend. Messrs Cook and Edwards of Bridgend are the architects and they are to be congratulated on the excellent arrangement of the new theatre and the beautiful design so well carried out.'

The advertisement float for D.W. Griffith's *White Rose, c.* 1924. Seated on the float, from left to right: Winnie Jenkins, Don Cunningham (projectionist at the cinema), Gwyneth Hopkin, Gladys Griffiths, and Mollie Jenkins. All the girls in the float lived in Elder Street and in time all went to work in the cinema.

The front of the float with Joe Redman holding the horse. To Joe's right is his youngest son Jack. The Redman family lived for many years at No 11 Elder Street. Looking around the pillar is John Griffiths from No 9 Elder Street and to the left of the picture, Jack and Bert Jenkins from No 3 Elder Street.

Left: 'The Cinema' under new management as advertised in the *Glamorgan Gazette* Friday 30 July 1915. Right: Alf Bresner (projectionist), Mrs Price (morning staff), Doris Redwood (Manageress), and local man Joey Brass, early 1920s. In May 1933, George Isaac took over the management of the cinema. At about this time, the cinema was completely refurbished inside and out and sound was installed by Western Electrics Ltd.

Staff from the three cinemas, Embassy, 'Cinema' and Palace attending a fire drill in 1940.

Cinema Staff, *c*. 1950. From left to right, back row: Joyce Kenwood, Grace Ashong, Manager Eric Evans, Gladys Smith, Nancy Davies. Front row: Margaret Meadows, Mavis Reynolds, Pauline Fletcher, Betty Vaughan.

Before a show at 'The Cinema', Cross Street, *c*. 1950. From left to right: Donald Houston (actor), Councillor Bill Ellis, Clifford Evans (actor) and Eric Evans (Cinema Manager).

Jo. Jones, newsagent and tobacconist, Cross Street, *c.* 1912.

Joseph Jones and friend, late 1920s.

The staff and their guests from the Cinema and Palace at their annual Christmas Dinner held at Conti's Café, early 1950s. Mr George Isaac is standing second from right. Another well known person is local hairdresser Harold Fisher, seated second from right.

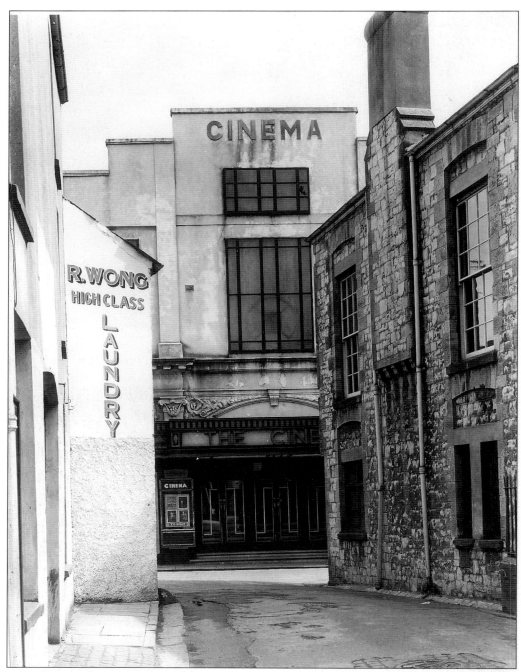

'The Cinema' (1912-1980) with the Chinese Laundry to the left and the Wyndham Hotel to the right. On 7 Sept 1980 after the last showing of the film *Can't Stop the Music*, the cinema finally closed its doors. It was demolished a short time after for town centre re-development and the site was occupied by an unloading bay. 'If not demolished, what a wonderful theatre and town museum the Cinema would have made.' (Quote from members of the Bridgend Civic Trust)

John Jenkins and his son David, c. 1900, outside their grocery and hardware shop, No 3 Cross Street.

Beryl Jenkins outside Conti's Café, Cross Street, late 1940s. This was also known as the 'Cinema Café'. Beryl's father and grandfather ran the grocery and hardware shop.

Conti's Café, late 1940s, before refurbishment.

Conti's Café, early 1950s, after refurbishment. The little girl is Patricia Ferrari.

Elder Street, 1955. This view shows the rear of the cinema, which was formerly the stables belonging to D.E. Evans, ironmongers, Dunraven Place, the horses being cared for by Harry Hiscocks who worked for D.E. Evans for 57 years. Much later, Fred and his wife Elizabeth Dunlop opened a DIY shop there, living above the shop with their two children, Roy and Joan. Mrs Dunlop remembers starting off the business with 'a shilling in the till'. The petrol pump to the right was selling Regent fuel.

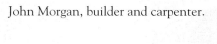
John Morgan, builder and carpenter.

Jane and David Morgan.

The wooden building to the left belonged to the brothers, David and John Morgan, who started their carpentry business there around 1885. Their sons Charlie and Len carried on the business after them. Later, Len started his own business at Sunnyside and Charlie carried on in Elder Street until his death in 1949.

Roy and Joan Dunlop with Jack Bowen who worked for the Dunlops for a time, mid-1930s.

The Morgan brothers were builders of the Wooden Bridge (Sankey's Bridge). This view from c. 1950 shows Angel Street on the left and the rear of Queen Street on the right with the Wooden Bridge in the distance.

Five

The Ship, the Wyndham and Dunraven Place

View of Dunraven Place looking north. The Ship Hotel to the right of the photograph, showing the tall stone pillars, low walls and iron railings. The horse chestnut trees were felled in the late 1930s to make way for the modernisation and extension to the Ship Hotel. Barclays Bank (formerly the London Provincial and South Western Bank) is on the left. On the right-hand side of the bank stands London House, the drapers.

David and Alice Hughes, pictured here in the early 1940s, were licensees of the Ship from 1935 until 1950.

Members of the '94 Club' photographed before a performance of *The Guinea Pig* at the Town Hall. The '94 Club', an amateur dramatic group was formed at the Ship about 1946. The group is now known as the Castle Players. Vernon Hughes (standing second from right) lived at the Ship at the time and was one of the founder members of the group.

View of the Ship Hotel *c.* 1955. The entrance and balcony to the left of the photograph were part of the 1930s extension. In the background are the side and rear entrances to the Cinema. Formerly known as the Ship Inn, this establishment has existed since the mid-eighteenth century. It was well known in the mid-nineteenth century as a coaching and posting inn. William Stephens, landlord of the Ship *c.* 1830, made his inn 'replete with every convenience' and provided 'good wines and genuine spirits, good stables with lock-up coach house'. The mile marker which stood just outside the gates was erected in 1836. The Ship was reputed to have the ghost of a coachman who was injured during a journey to Bridgend and died later in the building.

View of the Ship Hotel 1977. By this time the days were already numbered for the Ship. It was closed as a public house in 1980 to make way for re-development in the area. The Ship was a centre-piece in Dunraven Place and was always well kept.

On the right, David Ward, the last landlord of the Ship Hotel. On the left, well known local butcher Bernard Oakes. Next to him Eileen Quinn (*née* Murphy) born and brought up in the Kings Head, Nolton Street. The picture was taken *c*. 1979.

An unknown innkeeper, family and staff at the Wyndham Arms, around the turn of the century.

The Wyndham Hotel, c. 1906. The right of the building was formerly two houses and a small shop before being incorporated into the Wyndham Hotel. The cellar is said to have a tunnel leading down to the river.

An advertisement from the 'Borough' guide to Bridgend, 1910.

The Wyndham Hotel, 24 October 1935. The Wyndham Hotel staff and a visiting group of policemen who called themselves 'The Wyndham Boys'.

The Wyndham Hotel 1977. A grade two listed building, formerly called the Wyndham Arms, this is an old hostelry, dating back to the eighteenth century (around 1792). At one time part of the building was a Court House and Gaol. In 1830 the coach to London, 'The Regulator' (from Swansea) called at the Wyndham Arms every Monday, Wednesday and Friday mornings at a quarter before seven, making the return journey on Tuesdays, Thursdays and Saturdays. In 1983 a sixteenth century Sutton stone arch doorway was found in an internal dividing wall on the first floor of the hotel. It was confirmed to date from *c.* 1550 or earlier, indicating that a substantial building once stood on this site.

Dunraven Place, with the Wyndham Hotel standing in the background, March 1980.

Dunraven Place, 1950, looking north. On the left is London House which for well over a hundred years was a draper's shop in the town. In 1978 the business closed and the building was demolished. The clock you can see jutting out from the jewellers shop (Mason & Williams) was erected by Mr L. Beha at the end of the last century. His jewellery business was referred to as the 'shop under the clock'.

Mr Glyn Stephens' Music Shop, Dunraven Place, *c.* 1960. As well as selling records and sheet music for many years, Mr Stephens also taught music. He started his business in Dunraven Place in the early 1950s, retiring in 1974.

A copy of a deposit account from the London Provincial and South Western Bank (Barclays Bank) Dunraven Place, 1920.

The War Memorial floodlit. Designed by Walter Cook and sculpted from Portland stone by Messrs H.H. Martyn and Co. Ltd of Cheltenham, it was unveiled on 11 November 1921.

The War Memorial, looking east of Dunraven Place, late 1920s. To the right and above, the lights of the popular 'Café Royal'.

Six

'Our Magnificent Town Hall'

General William Booth, the founder of the Salvation Army, addressing a large crowd outside the Town Hall during his visit to Bridgend, c. 1910. General Booth is on the left standing in a carriage.

Built in 1844-1845, the Town Hall was designed by David Vaughan, a local architect. It was paid for by public subscription and was one of the very few Greek revival buildings in Wales. The entrance front comprised of a portico of four giant Doric columns with pediments above. The side elevations were of two storeys and the building was faced with cement. Inside at first floor level was an elegant assembly room with a coved ceiling and fine cornice. Housed there at various times were the police station, the County Court and the library.

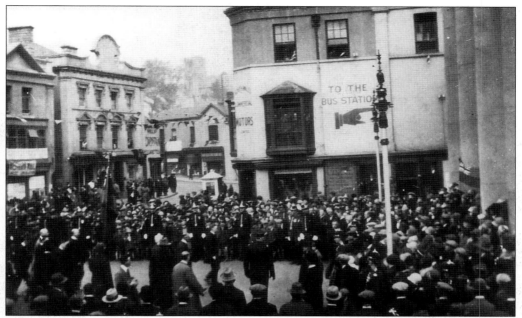

Dunraven Place in the early 1920s. Judging by the flags and bunting, it could easily have been a celebration, but of what, it has not been established. The hand on the wall points to Bridgend's very first bus station, which was situated directly behind the Town Hall. It was built by South Wales Commercial Motors.

Dunraven Place 1956. Look how narrow Market Street was!

It is 1969 and the days are now numbered for the Town Hall, completely engulfed in scaffolding. In 1970 it was put up for auction and failed to reach the reserve price of £40,000.

The Hall was eventually sold to a London-based construction company for £30,000. Sadly, and amid great controversy, we lost our Town Hall to the demolition men. What has become of the many paintings that hung in the great assembly room?

Seven
Bridges
and aerial views

This photograph from c. 1962 shows Bridge House to the right and also the rear of Angel Street. The new bridge in the foreground was built in 1912 replacing the original bridge of 1821. The new bridge (also known as the Embassy Bridge) is soon to be demolished and replaced by a modern footbridge.

The medieval stone bridge, floodlit in 1937, as part of the local celebrations of the coronation of George VI.

'Old Stone Bridge', c. 1970. The Embassy cinema to the rear of the photograph was opened in 1939. To the left, is the riverside walk which is now sadly no longer there.

Angel Street, 1920s, with the Cross Keys public house and Newcastle Hill in the background.

Aerial view of Bridgend town, late 1950s.

Aerial view of Bridgend town centre, late 1950s.

Eight
Wyndham Street, Caroline Street and Adare Street

Wyndham Street, early 1960s, On the right is the 'Wyndham of Wales' furniture shop, which ceased trading in 1966. Next door is Ivor Edwards' butchers, then a small café which later became a ladies hairdressers and on the left of picture the Ruhamah Welsh Baptist Chapel built in 1890.

Advertisement for Thompson and Shackell Ltd which was placed in the *Glamorgan Gazette* in 1913.

Demolition of No 1 Wyndham Street, 1966-67. The Trustee Savings Bank was built on the site.

After the demolition of the Wyndham of Wales furniture shop, a well was discovered.

Joe Black, grocery shop, No 10 Wyndham Street (next door to the library), early 1930s. Winnie Hack is in the centre.

The Darby and Joan Club and WVS, mid-1940s. The meeting hall was situated on the site of the first bus station between Wyndham Street and Market Street. Miss Hilda Roberts, a stalwart of the WVS, is seated third from left in the front row.

J.A. Jenkins, chemist, No 21a Wyndham Street, 1930s.

Flag day for the Darby and Joan Club took place each year in the first week of October. Here we see Gladys Price and Tom Price (no relation) dressed as Darby and Joan selling flags in the 1940s.

A view of the
upper end of
Wyndham street
taken in 1961.
Written on the
back of this
photograph is
'Congestion in
Wyndham
Street'. No
change there!

Adare Street, c. 1904, facing south. On the right-hand corner is George Singer, ironmongers.
He ran this business until about 1914. Although the shops on the left of the photograph have
changed greatly, the upper floors to some are still visibly the same. In 1922, F.W. Woolworth
replaced H. Woodward and Co. Woolworth's first manager was a Mr Grey.

George Singer (1846-1938). He was born at Newton Nottage, Porthcawl, the eldest son of Joseph and Mary Singer (*née* Lill). George's mother was the first landlady of the Red Lion public house in Elder Street. George was brought up by his grandparents, Joseph and Sarah Singer at the Victoria public house in Adare Street.

Advert from the *Glamorgan Gazette* at the turn of the century.

Above: the staff of F.W. Woolworth at a Christmas party, c. 1932. Below: the staff in 1954. The gentleman seated in the middle wearing glasses is the then manager, Mr Hewitt.

Lloyds Bank (formerly George Singer, ironmongers), c. 1955. A branch of Lloyds Bank was opened in Adare Street c. 1902 under the management of Mr William Watkins. Capital and Counties opened their branch opposite in 1914 and their manager was Mr Frederick R. Baker. In March 1919, the two branches merged to make Lloyds Bank Ltd. In 1931 the opening hours were from 10 a.m. to 3 p.m. Mondays to Fridays and 9.30 a.m. to 12 noon on Saturdays. The annual rent on the property was £200 with the premises rented initially on a short-term lease. The lighting was electric but there was no heating bar a coal fire in the manager's office. The staff numbered eight male clerks plus the manager. A cash point was installed inside the bank in 1974 and in April 1979 a 'through-the-wall' cash point was installed outside.

The National Provincial Bank, 28 Adare Street, 1894. The waste ground in the foreground previously sited a cattle and livestock market. The bank moved from their first premises in Eastgate Street (now Caroline Street) to their new position in Adare Street sometime after 1846. The first manager at the branch was Thomas George Smith 'the Elder'. He was succeeded as manager by his son Thomas George Smith 'the Younger', who did not retire until 1908. Up to the present day, the Adare Street bank has seen sixteen managers.

The Masonic Hall, 1977. This was constructed in 1891 and at one time this housed the 'Civic Restaurant'. Right of picture is the Tabernacl Welsh Independent Church with its facade of Quarella stone. The Tabernacl was built in 1850 and was demolished in 1986 to be replaced by four modern red-brick shops.

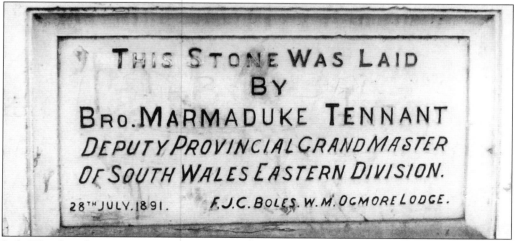

THIS STONE WAS LAID
BY
Bro. MARMADUKE TENNANT
DEPUTY PROVINCIAL GRAND MASTER
OF SOUTH WALES EASTERN DIVISION.

28TH JULY. 1891.   F. J. C. BOLES. W. M. OGMORE LODGE.

Left: This foundation stone was placed between the two doors of the Masonic Hall.

Tabernacl Welsh Congregational Church, Adare Street, 1977. Work commenced on this building in 1850 and the new church and was completed and opened in the autumn of 1851.

Tabernacl Hall, Elder Street, 1977.

The first Welsh Congregational Independent Chapel had been in Elder Lane (Elder Street) and was dedicated for service on 5 May 1810. Revd William Jones was the first minister and remained so for nearly forty years. He was not a native of Bridgend Town, but his long residence here, together with the fact that it was here that he produced his great work, caused him to be known as William Jones, Penybont-ar-Ogwr. A tall man with a strong personality, he was well versed in Hebrew, Greek, Latin, English and particularly in Welsh. He was an ardent advocate of Welsh language education. After a short illness in June 1847, Revd Jones died and was buried a few days later in Tabernacl churchyard. As a mark of respect to a great minister, all the shops in the town were closed on that day. When Tabernacl moved to bigger premises in Adare Street, the old chapel became a successful school for ministers under the leadership of Revd J. Bowen Jones B.A. The school remained open for approximately ten years. Some years later after the school had finally closed its doors, the old Chapel fell into disrepair and remained derelict until just before the outbreak of the Great War when the Chapel was rebuilt at a cost of over £1,000. The building was finally completed in 1917 and was opened by Alderman T.W. David of Cardiff, a former student at the school. Tabernacl Hall as it is now called, proved to be a great advantage to the work of the Chapel and the Sunday school.

Tabernacl Senior Sunday school, outside the Hall in Elder Street, July 1955.

Tabernacl Junior Sunday school, outside the Hall, 1955.

Bridgend   Adare Street

Two views of Adare Street. Above: at the turn of the century with the White Lion Hotel to the right. At this time, William Pitt was the proprietor. It ceased to be a public house in the early 1930s. Below: with the Victoria Hotel visible on the left, *c.* 1929. Formerly a Georgian house, this is one of the few pubs left in town to retain its original name.

Adare St. Bridgend. 536.

Leslie's store opened in Adare Street *c.* 1939. Looking at the centre window, you could buy a pair of ladies court shoes for 32s 6d. when this photograph was taken in the late 1950s.

Davies, the hat shop, the 'Leading Milliners', No 4 Adare Street *c.* 1933. This was formerly the White Lion public house.

Evan John outside his outfitters shop, 'Regent House', No 1 Adare Street, 1929. Mr John stands at the entrance of his shop which he established *c*. 1895 and continued to run until his death in 1941 aged 67 years.

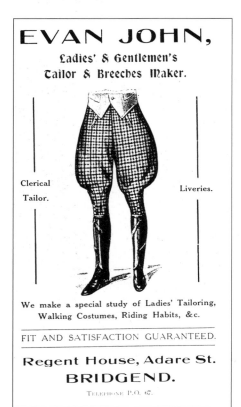

Advert taken from the 'Borough' guide, 1910.

The Adare Restaurant, 1957. October 1954 saw the arrival of the popular Fecci family in Adare Street. Brothers Gildo, Tony and their younger sister Irene.

Interior view of the Feccis' restaurant in Adare Street, looking to the rear, 1957.

Interior of the Adare Restaurant looking towards the entrance, 1957.

Glyn Jenkins, at the entrance of his shop not long before his retirement in 1988. Glyn T. Jenkins took over No 6 Adare Street from J.L. Stradling in the 1940s. Finally on 12 March 1994, this, the last independent grocery shop in the town centre closed its doors.

The 'full height shelving', draws and tea bins were amongst the Victorian fittings maintained in the interior of Glyn Jenkins' shop.

Note the marble topped counter.

The Brewer family at the turn of the century. From left to right, unidentified delivery man, brothers Albert junior, Edgar and Evan Brewer, Aunt Emma, sister to Albert senior, a nanny/maid (name unknown) who is holding the youngest son Charles. In the doorway of the shop, Sarah-Ann and Albert Brewer. Farmer Albert Brewer opened his shop at 13 Adare Street c. 1896. Together with his four sons, he ran a successful family business for many years. In later years, the family residence above the shop became offices, being used by a firm of solicitors and latterly by the Member of Parliament for Bridgend, Win Griffiths.

Two of Albert and Sarah's grandchildren, Mary Brewer and behind her cousin David with the family dog Prince, 1930s. The Tabernacl Church is in the background.

This photograph was taken during the General Election campaign of 1992. In July 1994 the building was demolished to make way for a building society.

The Victoria public house. A late Georgian three-storey building, formerly a large house, it became an inn around 1851. From 1935 until 1958, Bill and Bessie Davies were the licensees. Here we see Mr Bill Davies pulling pints in the bar of the 'Vic'.

Third from right is Mrs Bessie Davies with friends on a licensed victuallers annual outing in the 1940s. The young boy on the right is the Davies' only son, Billy, affectionately known as 'Billy the Vic'.

In 1973 Adare Street became a pedestrian-only precinct on Saturdays only.

The interior of Comer's Café at 9 Adare Street, *c.* 1939. Mr Comer opened his café here on the corner of Adare Street and Elder Street, in 1931-32, firstly as an ice-cream parlour and then as a restaurant. The business was sold in 1947 although the shop kept its name for many years.

An advertisement for Comer's.

Elder Street in 1956 with 'Comer's Café' on the right. The building behind (part of the Wyndham Yard) housed a blacksmith's.

Bevan & Lloyd,
BRIDGEND.

High-class Grocers,
Provision Merchants and
Italian Warehousemen.

ESTABLISHED OVER HALF A CENTURY.

43

Advert taken from the 'Borough' guide, 1910.

Dray outside the Castle Hotel, *c.* 1895. Tom Morgan is second from right.

Right: Caroline Street looking east, *c.* 1906. On the right the new market had just been completed. The Cottage Hospital, built in 1896 can just be seen at the top of the photograph on the right-hand side of the trees.

Caroline Street, turn of the century. This street was formally called Eastgate Street and was renamed after the dowager Countess of Dunraven. The post office is on the right and towards the middle is the entrance to the first market in Caroline Street established in 1837.

J. Jones (also known as Jones and Lewis), cash chemist, 29-31 Caroline Street, *c.* 1926.

From the 'Borough' guide, 1910.

Stokes & Company, clothiers and outfitters, Monmouth House, Caroline Street, Christmas 1926. From left to right: Harold Evans, Edwin Hunt (assistant), W.A. Stokes. The business was originally opened by a gentleman called Mr East in the 1850s. Mr H.J. Stokes took over the business as a going concern in 1896, followed by his son W.A. Stokes, then finally by his grandson, A.J. Stokes who in 1980 retired from the outfitting trade. The building is now occupied by a ladies' dress shop.

SELLING OUT AT COST

STOKES & SONS
Great Winter
SALE

In order to meet the urgent demand for Reduced Prices we are making Sweeping Reductions on all our Stock. You can rely on our word, this will be the Greatest Money Saving Event we have yet held. The Genuine Character of our SALES are well known. ... DON'T MISS THIS GREAT OPPORTUNITY.

OVERCOATS, RAINCOATS and SUITS

Offered at Enormous Reductions for Men, Youths and Boys.

Special Bargains as advertised; Jersey & Jersey Suits, Shirts, Underwear, Socks, Pullovers, Hats and Caps, etc.

SEE WINDOWS.   COME IN CROWDS.

STICK TO THE OLD FIRM **STOKES & SONS,** Caroline Street, Bridge

Advertising a January sale in 1928.

A.J. Stokes and W.A. Stokes, outside their shop, *c.* 1947.

Stokes & Sons, 1960. The interior of the shop had a solid block wooden floor.

The Bridgend Festival, September 1974. Mr A.J. Stokes is standing in the entrance of his shop.

The rear of Stokes & Sons, 1980, in the upper end of Elder Street. The roof of the bicycle shed is on the right.

Constance Stuchbery seated second from right on an annual outing with her staff, early years of this century. Miss Stuchbery established her draper's, millinery and dressmaking business in 1871 at the age of 21. Her nephew, Tom Price, became a partner with the firm in 1911 along with Joe Godsell, who had joined the firm at the turn of the century as an apprentice. Around the middle 1920s, Constance suffered a stroke and was unable to return to work. Her nephews continued to run the business until it closed in early 1972.

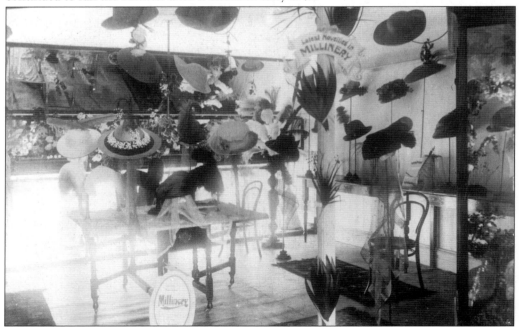

The millinery department on the first floor of Stuchbery's, Emlyn House, Caroline Street. The staff, dressmakers, milliners, counter hands and apprentices lived in the house next door to the right of the shop.

Exterior of Stuchbery's early 1900s. The shop also boasted a Lamson and Paragon 'cash railway'.

A receipt from
10 March 1908.

Advertisement for C. Stuchberry [sic], 1910.

Nine
Bridgend Market Hall (1906-1971)

The provision market was erected in Caroline Street and was entirely reconstructed in 1906. In April 1955, Bridgend Urban District Council purchased the Market Hall from the Dunraven Estates. Two archways and heavy wooden swing doors led to the spacious interior hall. Down both sides were many butchers stalls. Halfway down one side, a biscuit stall displayed many different varieties sold from open tin containers stacked neatly side by side inside a sliding glass window. There were several open fruit and vegetable stalls and Wilson's hosiery stall stood in the middle of two of these just inside the entrance. Delicatessen stalls stocked laver bread, cockles and trays of eggs stacked precariously on wooden trestle tables. In the centre, there was a china and glass stall. To the side of the china was a stall selling carpets and rugs. Peacocks had two stalls where Mrs Binds was manageress for over 40 years. Mr Henson's DIY stall occupied a stall to the left. Opposite, a gentleman, always dressed in a dark suit, sold bibles and prayer books. Another stall sold flowers, plants, bulbs and everything that was needed for the garden. A curtain and fabric stall was across on the right-hand side. Next door, the market café sold the best faggots and peas in town. Miss Iris Hay's sweet stall was opposite and at the top of the hall was a pet food stall with its many open sacks, displaying various dog biscuits etc. To the right of this and near the rear entrance to Queen Street stood Hawkins' fresh fish stall.

Interior view of the Market Hall, *c.* 1910.

Three Market butchers *c.* 1929: David George Davies, Bridgend; Griff Rees, Laleston; and John Francis, Coychurch, pictured at the rear entrance of the Market near the Rhiw.

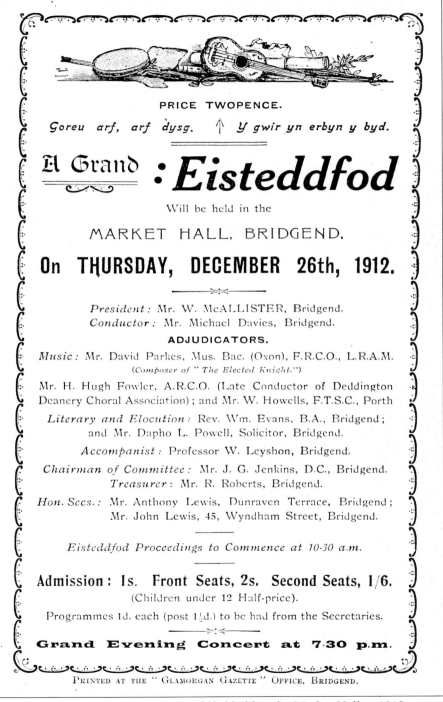

PRICE TWOPENCE.

Goreu arf, arf dysg. ↑ *Y gwir yn erbyn y byd.*

𝔄 Grand : *Eisteddfod*

Will be held in the

MARKET HALL, BRIDGEND.

On THURSDAY, DECEMBER 26th, 1912.

President : Mr. W. McALLISTER, Bridgend.
Conductor : Mr. Michael Davies, Bridgend.

ADJUDICATORS.

Music : Mr. David Parkes, Mus. Bac. (Oxon), F.R.C.O., L.R.A.M.
(Composer of " The Elected Knight.")

Mr. H. Hugh Fowler, A.R.C.O. (Late Conductor of Deddington Deanery Choral Association) ; and Mr. W. Howells, F.T.S.C., Porth

Literary and Elocution : Rev. Wm. Evans, B.A., Bridgend ; and Mr. Dapho L. Powell, Solicitor, Bridgend.

Accompanist : Professor W. Leyshon, Bridgend.

Chairman of Committee : Mr. J. G. Jenkins, D.C., Bridgend.
Treasurer : Mr. R. Roberts, Bridgend.

Hon. Secs. : Mr. Anthony Lewis, Dunraven Terrace, Bridgend ; Mr. John Lewis, 45, Wyndham Street, Bridgend.

Eisteddfod Proceedings to Commence at 10-30 a.m.

Admission : 1s. Front Seats, 2s. Second Seats, 1/6.

(Children under 12 Half-price).

Programmes 1d. each (post 1½d.) to be had from the Secretaries.

Grand Evening Concert at 7·30 p.m.

PRINTED AT THE " GLAMORGAN GAZETTE " OFFICE, BRIDGEND.

The front cover of a programme of an eisteddfod held in the Market Hall in 1912.

An invitation meet at the Three Horse Shoes, 1950s, showing the rear of the Market in the background and the Dunraven Yard to the back right.

Inside the Market Hall showing the high roof. The clock on the right always kept good time.

Front view of the Market early 1960s. The building to the extreme right was the Tennis Court public house.

View of the left-hand side from the entrance on Caroline Street, 1969-70.

Looking down towards the entrance in Caroline Street, 1969-70.

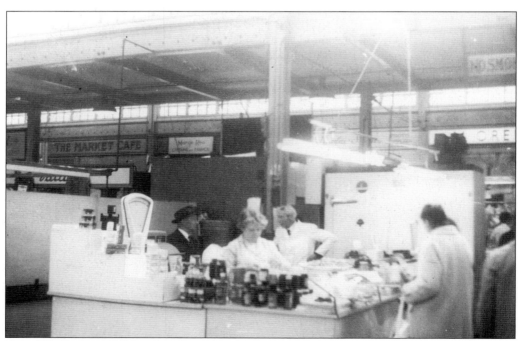

Nora Whalley and Bill Binds at the delicatessen, 1969-70.

The centre China stall, 1969-70. Note that the aisles were quite wide.

Peacocks, 1969-70. Mrs Binds was manageress here, running three stalls in the Market for over forty years.

The entrance to the Market, during the last week of shopping there, 8-13 May 1971. As indicated, the new market opened on Monday 15 May. The entrance was off Nolton Street. The two 'Dunraven Coat of Arms' on either side of the arch were a set of four. The other two were above the arch at the other entrance. Three were presumably smashed at the time of demolition. One was saved and is now on view at Bridgend Rugby Club.

A front view of the Market awaiting demolition, May 1971. The clock, made of slate with solid brass numerals, disappeared during the demolition but the bell and cupola were stored in the Bridgend Council depot at Free School Court. In 1986 the bell was removed to a Council yard in Maesteg where it lay forgotten until 1994. Then the Bridgend Civic Trust set about the task of bringing it back to home to Bridgend. The following year the Civic Trust found a sympathetic ear in Chartwell Land who now owned the Rhiw Shopping Centre. Finally on St David's Day, 1996, amid pomp and ceremony, the bell in its original wooden housing – now sparkling white – was unveiled by the Mayor of Ogwr.

Interior of the Market, shortly before demolition, 1971.

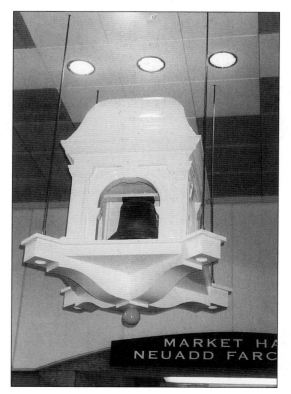

March 1st 1996. The Old Market bell and cupola hanging in 'pride of place' at the entrance to the Rhiw Shopping Centre. This was a fitting resting place for an object that has shared so much in the history of our market town.

Ten

The Flood Disaster
of 1960

After a few days of continual rain, the River Ogmore unexpectedly burst its banks at approximately 4 a.m. on Sunday 4 December 1960. It spilled over into the town centre, rapidly engulfing the low-lying streets with filthy water. Many residents were marooned and traders' premises ruined. Late afternoon, the water subsided leaving several inches of thick sludge. Householders and traders were then faced with the heartbreaking task of assessing the damage and cleaning up.

Adare Street, midday. By this time the water had already started to subside.

Dunraven Place, with the Wyndham Hotel to the left of the photograph. Along Queen Street and Dunraven Place the water was at its highest between four and five feet.

Dunraven Place looking towards Wyndham Street.

From Queen Street looking north. The mini seen in the centre of the photograph started to drift away, and had to be secured to a lamp standard by a few of the owner's neck ties.

The Embassy Bridge, 9 a.m., Sunday 9 December. The century-old wall in the foreground held up well to the flooded river.

Bridgend Fire Brigade pumping out in Dunraven Place.

Eleven
And finally…

Harry Lane pictured with his daily catch of rats. Around 1910 Harry lived at Glan-y-Ewenny Lodge and worked for the Turbervil family as gardener and coachman. About 1920 he left Glan-y-Ewenny to live in Angel Street with his wife Priscilla and two daughters, Agnes and Nellie. He was employed by Bridgend Urban District Council as the rat catcher until he retired in 1950. In the background you can see the old wooden cooling towers of the Electric Light Company in the Council yard at the bottom of Edward Street.

Mr Percy Sutton, pictured in the large saddlery and leather repair work room above Sutton & Davies, saddler's shop at the top of Wyndham Street, *c.* 1950. This shop had been established in 1891 by Mr John Lewis and he remained in charge of the business, John Lewis Saddlers, until 1949 when he decided to retire at the age of 80. He offered the business to his loyal friend and employee, Percy Sutton who took over the business along with his son-in-law Llyfrwy Davies, hence Sutton & Davies. Mr Sutton continued to work in the saddlery until he was 83, retiring in 1962 because of ill-health. About 1968 Mr Davies also decided to retire and the shop was finally closed after 77 years.

Sutton & Davies, saddlers, at the top end of Wyndham Street, 1949.

The Mitre Hotel, Caroline Street, 1960s (before the extension of Boots Chemist) with its very distinctive bottle-green tiled frontage.

Tom and Mary Murphy with four of their six children. From left to right: Reg, Maggie, Tom jnr. and baby Christopher. Tom Murphy came to Bridgend from Ireland in 1898, at the age of 19. He worked in the Angelton where he met his wife, Mary McGrath and he later kept a barber shop in Derwen Road until the outbreak of the First World War. Subsequently, he became landlord of the King's Head in Nolton Street where he stayed for 44 years until his death in 1962 at the age of 83.

Edward Loveluck (1879-1955), pictured here in 1954.

Edward Loveluck with the 1st Earl Jellicoe (Admiral and commander of the grand fleet, 1914-16) and Countess Jellicoe (with flowers) at the opening of the United Services Club in Bridgend.

Edward Loveluck was born on 4 December 1879, the eldest son of Charley Loveluck and Martha, daughter of Thomas Thomas. Edward left school at the age of 10 to work in the office of P.J. Thomas, architect. From this lowly beginning he raised himself through hard work becoming a chartered surveyor and qualified architect, top of his year in design when he sat the exam. Later in life he became interested in Town and Country Planning and was one of the prime movers in this field in Wales.

Throughout his life Edward Loveluck was a dedicated public servant. He was a member of the Bridgend Urban District Council from 1913 to 1925 and Chairman (1916-17, 1919-1923). During his time on the Council he did a great deal for the town. Due to his initiative as Chairman of the Housing and Planning Committee the first Council housing estate was built after he had persuaded the Minister of Health to make Bridgend a development area where it was necessary to erect houses. Work began on the first hundred houses in 1922 and 500 were eventually constructed without any cost to the ratepayers. A second great Loveluck-inspired scheme was the purchase by the Council of Newbridge Fields which subsequently became the recreation ground of Bridgend.

In 1925 Loveluck resigned from his Council work due to his other manifold commitments. In 1928 he was appointed a permanent Justice of the Peace for the County of Glamorgan and he served and chaired the Juvenile Court Panel. He was active over the years in several different organisations including the Boy Scouts, Bridgend and District and Porthcawl Naval Cadets, and the British Legion.

In 1955 the *Advertiser* reported the well-earned tribute paid to Loveluck by the Chairman of Bridgend UDC, Cllr D. Bellew. He was a 'man of justice... who spent endless hours doing work for the betterment of others...' (Janet Hearle)

Looking down Caroline Street during the 1974 Bridgend Festival.

The riverside walk, *c.* 1969.

Elder Street as it looked in 1977, with the Chinese Laundry and the Bakehouse take-away on the left, Wyndham Yard in the distance and the County Cinema to the right. The laundry was opened just after the Second World War in a building once occupied by the Red Lion public house and many a 'gentleman's' collar was washed, starched and pressed here. The Cinema was built where two cottages – Nos 5 and 7 Cross Street – had once stood. At the second of these John Doxsey ran a successful carriage manufacturing business.

All the hustle and bustle that once made this a lively heart for the town centre has now disappeared and the future of the street is in the balance. One's own optimism can only ride high!

Acknowledgements

The response I have received in both photographs and information over the last few years has undoubtedly been tremendous and I would like to thank the following people and organisations most sincerely for their support and encouragement in making this book possible:

My mother, Molly, Aunts Nancy and Winnie, my (late) Uncle Fred, Uncle Charles and my father-in-law Chris Murphy. Mrs Natalie Stiles, Mrs Gladys Ball, Miss Patricia Ferrari, Mrs J. Ferrari, Mrs Pat Webber, Mrs Hilary Thomas, Mrs Anne Williams, (the late) Jack Redman, Mrs Ruth Wriggley, Mrs Nan John, Mrs Sonya Bentley, Mrs N. Amos, Mr David Ward, Mr and Mrs Cliff Jones, Mrs Pat James, Mrs Kitty Rowe (née Lloyd), Mr and Mrs Vernon Stride, (the late) Mr F. McKenzie, Mr and Mrs H.M. Lloyd, Allan and Betty Saunders, Mrs Connie Jones, Mrs Pina Fecci, (the late) Mr George Isaac, Mr David Jenkins, Mrs Diana Wood, Mr Mike Stokes, Mr and Mrs H. Harries, Mrs E. Bowen, Mr L. Davies, Mrs Hilary Staiger, Mrs M. Humphrys, Mrs Barbara Miller (née Comer), Mr and Mrs Philip Vaughan, Mr Graham Collins, Mr Mark Alberd, Mr Peter Smith, Mrs Janice Thomas, Mr Llew Davies, Mrs Barbara Mountjoy, Mrs Rose Brinkley, Mrs Anne Davies, (the late) Mrs D. Griffiths, Mrs Wynne Griffiths, Mrs M. Stephens, Mrs Iris Walters, Mr Colin Evans, Mr Danny Murphy, Mrs Mary Phillips, Mrs Marlene Hibbert, Mrs Peggy Turner, Mr W. Davies ('the Vic'), The Chan family ('Wyndham Hotel'), Mrs Anne Morris, Peter and Gayle Woods, Margaret and Gwilym Rees, Philip Thomas, (the late) Mrs E. Dunlop, Mrs J. Williams, Mrs Beattie Hopkins, (the late) Mrs Doris Whiley, Mrs Marian Minchington, Mrs Anne Lewis, Mrs Nancy Watkins, Miss May Morgan, Mrs Audrey Hooper, Rob Hathaway, Mrs Trevor Jones, Mr and Mrs H. Harries, Mrs E. Bowen, Mr Vernon Hughes, Miss Alice Snow, Mr C. Dor, (the late) Mr Bobby Mayo, Mr Spencer Mayo, Mr Ron Jenkins, Mr L. Thomas, Mrs Beryl Wood, Mrs Daphne Jones, Mr John Jones, Mrs Pauline Bertorelli, Mrs Margaret Hughes, Mr Gordon Westcott, Mrs Pat Bevan-Morgan, Mr Derrick Brewer, Philip Marks, Mr Glyn Jenkins, Mid-Glamorgan County Libraries, Coed Parc, Margaret, Mary, Leslie, Robert and especially Hazel from Coed Parc and Wyndham Street libraries, Chartwell Land, Laleston Community Council, Ogwr Borough Council Planning Department, Jayne and Alec from the *South Wales Echo*, Jenny Walford from the *Western Mail*, the staff of the *Glamorgan Gazette*, the Earl of Dunraven, Lloyds Bank plc Archives, National Westminster Bank Group Archives, Mr David Pearce and Mrs Janet Hearle, Peter and Mary from 'Park Street Studios' for their patience and help.

Special thanks go to Hilary Rowley for her excellent introduction; to Charles Thorp for his part of the introduction and the word processing; Simon Eckley for his advice, guidance and patience; Mike Stokes for patiently reading the proofs, and lastly my husband David for his moral support. If anyone has been omitted from this list, it has not been intentional and I do apologise.